So, You're Moving to Asheville!

A Handbook to Being an Ashevillian

RUSSELL C WORDS

SO YOU'RE MOVING TO ASHEVILLE!...
A HANDBOOK TO BEING AN ASHEVILLIAN

Copyright 2017 by Russell C Words

All rights reserved. No part of this book may be reproduced or transmitted in any form or by any means, electronic or mechanical, including photocopying, recording or by any information storage and retrieval system without permission in writing from the Publisher.

Russell C Words
Flat Rock NC 28739

International Standard Book Number 978-1-935771-38-8

Moving to Asheville...

What's Up With...   5
   those things that make Asheville uniquely Asheville

Living in Asheville   35
   Celebrating around Asheville...
   Cheering around Asheville...
   Dogwalking around Asheville...
   Drinking around Asheville...
   Driving around Asheville...
   Eating around Asheville...
   Listening around Asheville...

The Towns Around Town...   61

Prologue

Best Small Cities in America. Best Cities for Beer Drinkers. Best Cities for Keeping Your Resolutions. Best Small Cities for a First Date. Coziest Cities in America. Best Foodie Destinations in the USA. Best Cities to Spend a Weekend. Best Places to Retire in the U.S. Top Towns for Craft Lovers. Friendliest Cities in the U.S. Best Small Town Family Weekend Destinations. Top 10 Fall Foliage Destinations. America's Greatest Music Cities. Top 5 Pet-Friendly Towns. Top Small City Arts Destinations. Most Romantic Cities in the South. Best Places to Live and Work as a Moviemaker. America's Smartest Cities. Quirkiest Towns. Dreamy Towns for Vegan Living. America's Best River Towns. Best Cities for Weight Loss. Fantastically Yoga Friendly Towns. Great Adventure Towns. Best Places to Reinvent Your Life.

Asheville has made all those lists. No wonder you are thinking of moving here. Or are moving or already have. Some eight million Americans move every year. Now, you're one of them. You've come to the right place.

In these pages you'll learn the explanations behind the quirks, the traditions and the secrets that make Asheville uniquely Asheville. *So You're Moving to Asheville!...A Handbook to Being an Ashevillian* will help you join the club in no time.

Why do Ashevillians love balds? Solved. The origin of Land of The Sky? A mystery no more. Samuel Ashe? Identified. The identity of the Pink Lady? Can't help you with that.

Celebrating in Asheville...Cheering in Asheville…Dogwalking in Asheville…Drinking in Asheville…Driving in Asheville...Eating in Asheville…Listening in Asheville. This book will have you speaking like a native in no time.

Because the next best thing to being a real Ashevillian is being able to pass as one.

What's Up With...
(those things that make Asheville uniquely Asheville)

What's Up With...Samuel Ashe?

There is no swashbuckling story of a visionary founder carving a town of destiny out of the wilderness for Asheville to hang its hat on. Samuel Davidson was the first non-native settler in these parts of the Blue Ridge Mountains, arriving with his family in the spring of 1784. Davidson and his wife Rachel built a cabin on Christian Creek in the Swannanoa Valley but he didn't live long enough to see the leaves change as he was killed in an Indian attack. His wife and child and a slave named Eliza escaped over the mountain to Davidson's Fort (Old Fort today) sixteen miles away. But Asheville was never named for Samuel Davidson.

The "Swannanoa Settlement" soon followed, led in part by Colonel David Vance and Davidson's brother, William. But Asheville was never named for either of them. In 1793 John Burton scored a state land grant and staked out 42 half-acre lots which anyone able to scrape together $2.50 in gold could buy. But he did not name the nascent community after himself. Instead, Burton called the settlement Morristown, after Robert Morris of Philadelphia, considered the "Financier of the American Revolution." At the time Morris owned the North American Land Company that controlled six million acres of land, including much of the Carolina frontier. That was more land than 13 of today's states; by comparison, today's North Carolina comprises 32 million acres.

It was too much even for Morris and he, at one time the richest man in America, wound up spending over 40 months in debtor's prison before being released to die as a pauper. Meanwhile, the Western North Carolina settlement named for Morris was being incorporated in 1797 without him. The town name was changed to honor the current governor, Samuel Ashe. Ashe was a lawyer from Cape Fear on the coast who was involved in North Carolina politics both under British rule and American rule. He was 70 years old in 1795 when he was elected to the first of three consecutive one-year terms. Ashe never visited his namesake town and about all he knew of western North Carolina was the headache caused by land fraud involving the formation of Tennessee in the final year of his administration.

There are no heroics in the origin of the name of Buncombe County, either. The honoree here is Edward Buncombe, a native of the West Indies who inherited a plantation along the Albemarle Sound. When he was 35 years old Buncombe was elected a colonel in the 5th North Carolina Regiment of the Continental Army and went off to serve under George Washington. He was never to return to the Old North State. During a disastrous battle (for the good guys) in Germantown, outside of Philadelphia on October 4, 1777, Colonel Buncombe was wounded and taken prisoner. The British paroled him but apparently while sleepwalking Buncombe tumbled down some stairs, broke open his healing wounds and bled to death. He was buried in Philadelphia in the same churchyard where Robert Morris would be interred 28 years later.

The county named for Buncombe was formed in 1792, cleaved off of Rutherford and Burke counties. But Western North Carolina did not cover the Buncombe name with glory. The representative it sent to the 16th Congress of the United States in 1820 was Felix Walker, a one-time trader and land speculator then 66 years old. In the Capitol that year Congress vociferously debated for a solid month the eventual epochal Missouri Compromise that preserved the balance of power between slave and free states. Walker sat silent through it all but just before the final vote he insisted on delivering a long, windy speech that added nothing to the debate. As he was shouted down by weary colleagues, Walker was reported to say, "I was just talking for Buncombe." The term "bunkum," later shortened to "bunk," quickly entered the popular lexicon as fatuous and irrelevant commentary. If only Edward Buncombe hadn't walked in his sleep…

What's Up With...The Land of The Sky?

When your stock in trade is selling your city to visitors, a catchy slogan can come in handy. Boosters of the Western North Carolina mountains began popping up after the Civil War, spreading word of the "healing springs and healthy climate" to outsiders. In 1876, a 29-year old native of Salisbury named Frances Fisher wrote a novel about her adventures growing up in "Mountains that like giants stand, sentinel enchanted land." Fisher, who crafted over 50 books under her pen name of Christian Reid, called her novel *The Land of the Sky*.

The name was an instant star. The first postcards and promotional brochures bearing painted images of the Land of the Sky began appearing as early as the 1880s. In short order hotels from Caesar's Head in South Carolina to Asheville were luring out-of-town guests to this magical place called "The Land of The Sky." When the Southern Railway began pushing track out of Charleston into the mountains the entire region - Flat Rock, Tryon, Saluda, Hendersonville and other points - was lumped into The Land of The Sky.

The Southern worked the slogan hard. The railroad published regular promotional guidebooks to the Land of The Sky and its copywriters tried to give each mountain town a beguiling personality. Asheville became the "Madonna of the Mountains." Saluda was "Charming, Healthful, Recuperative" and Flat Rock was "Historic and Exquisitively Picturesque." Waynesville was "A Natural Resort of Great Beauty and Fine Climate" and Hot Springs was "An Ideal Autumn and Winter Resort." Brevard resided "in the Exquisite Land of Waterfalls." Lake Toxaway was "A Wonder-spot of Scenic Beauty." And Hendersonville was the "Gem City of the Western North Carolina Mountains."

It was the Southern Railway that spread "The Land of The Sky" logo far and wide.

Over time Asheville appropriated the slogan and The Land of The Sky is now mostly associated with the city and not the region. And what became of Frances Fisher, who never actually mentioned Asheville in any of her adventures in the Western North Carolina mountains? She married a fellow named James Marquis Tiernan and moved to Mexico where he owned silver mines. There she wrote a novel called *Land of the Sun*.

Nothing could epitomize The Land of The Sky like the Biltmore mansion.

What's Up With...Grove This, Grove That?

There is an exquisite shopping arcade named for him, a fantastic hotel, an exclusive neighborhood, an historic golf course - who is this Grove who is everywhere in Asheville? Edwin Wiley Grove is sometimes called "The Father of Modern Asheville" but he was neither a native of Western North Carolina nor ever a full-time resident of the region. Grove was born in Hardeman County in Tennessee in 1850 and began his business career clerking in a pharmacy.

The "Father of Modern Asheville."

He bought the business in 1880, at a time when local pharmacists busily experimented with syrupy medicinal concoctions. That is how Coca-Cola started in 1886. At the same time, in his small Tennessee shop, Edwin Grove brewed a tasteless chill tonic with quinine that was used to treat the chills and fever of malaria. Grove's Tasteless Chill Tonic was a bigger hit than Coca-Cola, selling over a million bottles a year for decades.

Grove suffered from chronic bronchitis and rather than seek relief in one of his own medicine bottles he chose to retreat to the clean mountain air of Asheville for periods of recovery. At the time the town was famous for its restorative climate. There were dozens of sanitariums operating for tubercular patients - so many in fact that civic leaders feared Western North Carolina would be permanently branded a "health resort" rather than a "tourist resort."

Edwin Grove helped insure that would not happen. He made his first investment in Asheville in 1909, buying up 408 acres in the north end of town. Ironically, for a man who was lured to the region for its curative powers one of Grove's first acts was to buy several tubercular sanitariums and burn them down. When he was ready to open his Grove Park Inn he didn't want any rich vacationers to mistake the town for a patient ward.

It took crews of 400 men working 10-hour shifts, six days a week hauling granite boulders off Sunset Mountain to construct Grove's dream hotel. When it opened on July 12, 1913 the Secretary of State, William Jennings Bryan, was on hand to deliver the dedication speech. There had been grand hotels in Asheville before but the Grove Park Inn ushered in a new era of hospitality that cemented the region's reputation for high-style vacationing. The last sanitarium in town closed down in 1930.

Ten United States presidents have stayed in the Grove Park Inn since it opened in 1913.

Although Grove was also busily developing in Atlanta he was not through with Asheville. In 1926 he commissioned Charles Newton Parker to design one of America's last classic indoor shopping arcades. Parker tapped the Venetian Gothic style for the Grove Arcade that consumes an entire downtown block, sheathing the exterior in ivory-hued terra cotta tile. He placed a pair of winged lion sculptures to guard the northern entrance. Edwin Wiley died in 1927 and never saw the completion of Parker's masterpiece Neither did anyone else; the planned central 14-story office tower was never built. Today you can see a representation of the grand scheme for the arcade etched in glass on the northeast corner of Battery Park Avenue and Page Avenue.

So there are a lot of things named for Edwin Wiley Grove. Maybe the best is back in his home state of Tennessee where he endowed a free public high school. The students honored Grove by adopting the team nickname of the Chill Tonics.

What's Up With...
the World's Third Oldest River?

Western North Carolina was settled mostly by Scotch-Irish, many of whom drifted south out of Pennsylvania. French influences and cultural heritage are few and far between. There is Lenoir, named for William Lenoir of French Huguenot descent who served with distinction during the American Revolutionary in North Carolina. After the war he settled near the town that would take his name and lived in Wilkes County all the way until 1839. But not much more than that.

So how did Asheville's signature river become the "French" Broad River? The water gathers in southern Transylvania near the town of Rosman and heads northwest for 117 Western North Carolina miles before continuing into Tennessee where it helps create the Tennessee River and ultimately heads for the Mississippi River. Geologists tell us it is the third oldest river on earth - so old there weren't any organisms around to die, sink to the bottom and become fossils.

The French Broad River is not particularly broad - that was a generic name for rivers back in the day. Asheville is the largest of the 25 municipalities the river serves along the 117 miles it flows through North Carolina.

Apparently early settlers had a limited imagination for place names since there were two Broad Rivers in North Carolina. This one flowing through Asheville headed into territory controlled by France and became the "French Broad River." The Army Corps of Engineers showed up in the 1870s with plans to turn the French Broad into a navigable river but it didn't work. Today the vessels that ply the French Broad River are mostly canoes and kayaks and tubes meandering gently (most of the time) through the mountains.

But the waters are not without their hair-raising moments. The Siren of the French Broad has her origins in early Cherokee times and the gorgeous dark-haired temptress had her coming-out party in an 1845 poem. The Siren comes to male travelers on the river in visions, luring them to the water. They gaze at her beauty under the surface and inevitably reach down for her - at which moment the Siren's flesh turns scaly and she yanks the love-struck dupe to his watery doom.

North America's smallest turtle, the Bog Turtle, calls the French Broad River watershed home. The endangered amphibian grows no larger than this drawing and weighs only four ounces.

What's Up With...So Many Folks Imploring Helen to "Come Forth"?

Helen is a ghost. Asheville has a lot of ghosts. Start with close-knit families living in remote hollers and small towns for centuries, add Civil War lore and mix it all in a cauldron with Cherokee legends and you will no doubt end up with a potent spectral stew. No matter where you move in Western North Carolina chances are good you will be settling within shouting distance of an otherworldly spirit or two.

The Cherokee were the first people to live in the land that would become Asheville - or were they? Cherokee legend tells of a race of people they encountered when they arrived. Accounts differ about the Moon-Eyed People, as the Cherokee called them. These folks were either blind in the daylight and could only see in the dark or they were unable to see during certain phases of the moon. Either way, the Cherokee invaders completely annihilated the Moon-Eyed People. That is certain to create some restless spirits in the mountains.

Nothing gets the netherworld to stirring like the burning of old, rambling hotels. Hot Springs, located on the French Broad River, was one of the first resorts to develop in North Carolina's mountains. The Warm Springs Hotel was raised in 1837 and well-heeled guests traveled up the Buncombe Turnpike to dance in the state's largest ballroom and relax in the 108-degree natural springs. It burned in 1884, about the time an even hotter spring was discovered and the town was re-named Hot Springs. The Mountain Park Hotel was built and boasted 1,000 feet of piazzas. It lasted until a fire in 1920. The replacement Hot Springs Inn went up in flames in 1977. No wonder there have been ghost sightings in the tubs and cabins.

The fighting of the Civil War didn't much reach into Western North Carolina but the mountains are not without their scars. Start with the spectral sightings of a fiddle-picking Confederate soldier named Tom Dula (pronounced "Dooley"). Dula managed to survive the war and was released from a Union prison camp in 1865 to make his way back to his native Wilkes County. He was still not yet 21 with his whole life ahead of him. His freedom, however, would last scarcely a year, his life less than three.

Back in Reedy Branch Dula took up with an old girlfriend named Ann Foster, who had since married. He also found time for dalliances with two of her cousins, one of whom, Laura, ended up dead and buried in a roadside grave. Both Tom and Ann were arrested for murder, the motive being that Laura was responsible for infecting the lover's quartet with syphilis. Tom Dula ended up hanging for the deed although many thought he confessed to spare Ann who had done away with Laura out of jealousy.

Fast forward 90 years to an unknown group of folk singers calling themselves the Kingston Trio. They heard a version of the traditional Appalachian love-gone-wrong ballad in a San Francisco nightclub and recorded their own interpretation for their debut album. "Tom Dooley" sold six million copies and turned folk music into a commercial proposition. The following year Michael Landon starred as Tom Dula in a movie version of the tawdry tale. And Tom Dula's ghost? It is said to still haunt the jail in Statesville where the doomed lover spent his last days before being hanged in front of a raucous crowd of 3,000 onlookers.

Confederate soldier Tom Dula..."Poor boy, you're bound to die..."

But, back to Asheville. One of the city's early attractions was its clean air. Many sick people came for the restorative climate and many died. Chase P. Ambler was one who owned a tuberculosis sanitarium. A thirty-third degree mason, he also was instrumental in constructing the Neoclassical Scottish Rite Cathedral at the corner of Broadway and Woodfin Street in 1915. The brick Masonic temple was shortly pressed into duty as an emergency hospital during the deadly Spanish influenza of 1918. Today the temple is the hypocenter for paranormal explorations in Asheville.

The Jackson Building was the first skyscraper in Western North Carolina, erected in 1923-24. Its height has contributed to its reputation as one of the most haunted buildings in Asheville.

So grab your EMF meter (electronic-magnetic field detector) and start there before poking around the city. A few block aways on Pack Square sits perhaps the most haunted building in town. The slender Jackson Building on the southeast corner was the first skyscraper in Western North Carolina when it was topped off in 1924. It was raised on land owned by the father of author Thomas Wolfe until his death in 1922; next door the Westall Building was constructed by Wolfe's uncle.

Architect Ronald Greene draped the Neo-Gothic Jackson Building in terra cotta and crowned it with stone leopard gargoyles. The foreboding countenance proved prescient when the stock market crashed five years later. Stories began spreading of ruined businessmen leaping from office windows. It was so bad, the stories went, that hotel clerks would ask guests checking in if the room was for sleeping of jumping.

Over at the Grove Park Inn you will hear stories, perhaps conflicting, of the Pink Lady. The flesh and blood embodiment of the spirit was a woman from the 1920s, maybe beautiful and maybe a debutante but not famous like many of the inn's guests. She may have been murdered in the hotel. Possibly she plunged to her death in the interior courtyard. She may have been wearing a pink ballgown at the time of her death. Or she may never have existed at all.

But her spirit, a mist or fog really, is in residence today. She seems to prefer the winter and quieter times at the hotel to make her appearance. The Pink Lady's presence is most often reported in and around Room 545, manifesting itself as a cold chill in the air. Mostly she is reported as helpful to the staff and guests as she approaches a century in residence in the Grove Park Inn.

The ultimate case of a spirit in no hurry to retire from opulent surroundings is at the Biltmore.

Are these bowling lanes in the Biltmore mansion being used after hours?

George Washington Vanderbilt, heir to the Venderbilt shipping and railroad fortune, used part of his inheritance to build the largest private house in the United States in 1895. But he enjoyed his 250-room, French-flavored castle for less than two decades. After George Vanderbilt died unexpectedly from an appendectomy in 1914 at the age of 51, his wife Edith was often heard talking to him in the library. Later George was observed in the billiards room as well. Edith has apparently joined him in the house in the afterlife. She apparently favors the indoor pool where she was known to throw fabulous parties. Even the intrusion of the public into the much-visited Biltmore House has not dislodged the couple from their magnificent lair.

And so who was Helen? Her story is also cloaked in wealth. Zealandia is a Tudor Gothic castle that rises out of the solid granite of Beaucatcher Mountain, built in the early 1900s for Philip S. Henry, an internationally known diplomat and businessman. He named his new place after a cattle ranch in New Zealand that was the foundation of his fortune. Helen was a woman who lived nearby or on the estate. After her daughter died, either in a fire or from mysterious circumstances at Zealandia, the distraught mother hanged herself from an arched stone bridge built as a carriageway on the grounds.

To coax Helen's troubled spirit out of her hiding place, paranormal investigators call "Helen, come forth!" three times. If she does not appear it could be because she is messing with your vehicle - there have been reports out at Helen's Bridge of cars that mysteriously refuse to start for a return trip down the mountain.

In 1928 the Zealandia Castle on Beaucatcher Mountain was offered to President Calvin Coolidge as a summer White House. The Coolidges never moved in. Perhaps they heard something about the place being haunted.

What's Up With...the Heaviest Rainfall Ever Recorded in the United States?

When a hurricane threatens the East Coast the TV weatherpeople all rush to an unlucky coastal location with their rain slickers and umbrellas to document the destruction. But those big storms seldom stop at shore's edge. Asheville has seen its share of hurricanes, too.

Such was the case in July of 1916. A cyclone - hurricanes did not as yet have names - tore through the Gulf of Mexico and stalled on the crest of the Blue Ridge mountains, pouring rain down the slopes for six days. After a few days of clearing another hurricane came ashore north of Charleston and moved inland. The storm moved inland before banging into the mountains in Western North Carolina. Beginning on July 15 the corralled front unloaded 22.22 inches of rain - the heaviest 24-hour rainfall ever recorded in the United States at that time.

It was estimated that the saturated ground absorbed only 10 percent of the deluge. The Swannonoa River was said to be a mile wide and the French Broad engorged from 380 feet wide to 1,300 feet, a quarter mile. The waters crested at 21 feet, 17 feet above flood stage. The resulting floodwaters were responsible for more than 300 mudslides in Asheville alone and at least 80 people died. The washing away of topsoil crippled area farmers for years.

Can the Great Flood of 2016 happen in Asheville again? Probably not to that extent, thanks to advancements in stormwater management and warning systems. But the dangerous weather patterns remain. In 2004 Hurricanes Frances and Ivan marched into western North Carolina nine days apart and dumped up to 18 inches of rain in the mountains. Floods caused over $100 million in damage and took eleven lives.

And about that daily rainfall record? It has been broken, almost doubled in fact, by Alvin, Texas which endured 43 inches of rain in a 24-hour period in 1979 during Tropical Storm Claudette. Asheville's 22 inches is still the North Carolina record, even though in a typical year the city receives about 40 inches of rain, the fewest in the state.

What's Up With...Thomas Wolfe's Angel?

Many famous people come to live in Asheville, not so many start here. One of the first and most famous of Asheville native sons was Thomas Wolfe. Wolfe's debut novel in 1929, *Look Homeward, Angel*, was an international best-seller and propelled Wolfe into the front rank of American writers before he was 30 years old.

People in Asheville were not as thrilled. Wolfe's novel was a fictionalized account of growing up in his mother's rambling Victorian boarding house at 48 Spruce Street. Not everyone, including his family, believed Wolfe did a very good job at "fictionalizing" the more than 200 characters in the novel. The folks at the public library were so furious that *Look Homeward, Angel* was banned from the collection for seven years. For his part, Wolfe stayed away from his hometown until dying prematurely at the age of 37 in 1938.

Wolfe's mother continued to live in the house, called "Old Kentucky Home," until she died in 1945. The house became a museum four years later and is one of the most sought out literary landmarks in America. Meanwhile a dispute brewed over the identity of the titular angel.

Wolfe drew inspiration for the novel from an angel statue that stood on the family porch in Asheville. All parties involved agree on that. Problem is, Thom-

"Wolfe's Angel is located in Oakdale Cemetery in Hendersonville.

as Wolfe's father ran a funeral monument shop so there were a lot of statues hanging around. In fact, W.O. Wolfe had ordered a bunch of the Italian Carrera marble angels from a dealer in Pennsylvania. There was an angel in a cemetery in Old Fort, another in Bryson City and a third in Oakdale Cemetery in Hendersonville.

Which one was really Wolfe's "An Angel on the the Porch?" This was no small deal, especially as Wolfe's novel gained iconic status - it has never gone out of print since its publication almost 90 years ago. The various towns bickered over who had the real goods.

Thomas Wolfe's own grave is in Asheville's Riverside Cemetery.

It eventually got to be too much for Myra Champion, a Wolfe historian in the Pack Memorial Library, to bear. In 1949 she tracked down anyone from the past half-century who had anything to do with a marble angel in the Blue Ridge Mountains. Old Fort had the best story - old man Wolfe lost that one in a poker game. But in her definitive analysis Champion declared that the true Wolfe angel was in Oakdale, "marking the grave of Mrs. Margaret Bates Johnson, wife of the late Dr. H.F. Johnson, a minister and former president of Whitworth College in Brookhaven, Mississippi."

A slight departure from the grave of a young prostitute it marks in the novel. Apparently the tipping point in its identification stands on the Hendersonville angel's "phthisic foot" - the withered appendage, as described by Wolfe, that was the result of tuberculosis, the same disease that would also take the writer's life.

What's Up With...All the Movie Cameras?

Hollywood of the East. That is how movie folk talk about North Carolina. It all started back in the early 1980s when big shot Italian movie producer Dino De Laurentiis was looking for a Southern mansion to stand in for an elegant Virginia plantation in the screen adaptation of Steven King's *Firestarter*. De Laurentiis happened to see a photo of Orton Plantation in Brunswick County on the cover of a magazine and soon he was on a plane to North Carolina to shoot his movie with nine-year old ingenue Drew Barrymore in the lead. In addition to filming around Wilmington the production moved to Western North Carolina to shoot footage around Lake Lure and Chimney Rock.

After the crews were finished with *Firestarter* in 1984 everyone assumed De Laurentiis was through with the state. Instead, he stayed in Wilmington and constructed the largest television and movie production facility in America outside California. So many productions used North Carolina that it picked up that nickname as the "Hollywood of the East." It was not the first time the silver screen had been smitten with North Carolina in general and the mountains in particular.

At the dawn of the silent film era in 1914 the Edison Motion Picture Company began making short pictures in Western North Carolina. Thomas Edison, who had been summoned to Asheville years earlier to install an electric trolley, tipped off his movie company about the natural beauty of the region. Downtown Asheville and the surrounding countryside would be used as the backdrop for some 20 movies in the following years before almost all productions beat a retreat to the convenience of Hollywood sound stages in the 1920s.

When De Laurentiis rekindled Hollywood's interest in the Tar Heel State it did not take long for Western North Carolina to start piling up credits in classic movies. Lake Lure did its best impersonation of a 1950's Catskills, New York resort for *Dirty Dancing* in 1986. All of the famous interior dancing scenes - Baby carrying a watermelon and practicing with Johnny in his cabin - were filmed in an old boy's camp that is now Firefly Cove on the north side of the lake. Each summer since 2010 the town has celebrated its part in the movie by staging the

Dirty Dancing Festival.

Meanwhile, intrepid location scouts were discovering DuPont State Forest south of Asheville. It is "DuPont" because the massive chemical company bought 12,000 acres of pristine woodlands to manufacture sensitive X-ray film in crisp, clean air in the 1950s. The waterfalls of the forest along the Little River were tabbed to play New York State on the big screen for *The Last of the Mohicans*. Hooker, Triple, High and Bridal Veil Falls all took star turns in the Fenimore Cooper saga. So too did Hickory Nut Gorge at Chimney Rock State Park for the film's climax. But the most memorable waterfall scenes - with Daniel Day Lewis in a cave behind a pounding wall of water - were not shot in Western North Carolina, or anywhere else. You may hear folks tell you they were shot here but they were not. Day Lewis is pledging "I will find you" in front of computer generation.

Edith Taliaferro starred in the first feature film shot in Western North Carolina - **The Conquest of Canaan,** *released in 1916.*

The DuPont State Forest was also used as the backdrop in the wildly popular *Hunger Games* in 2012 as were many other Western North Carolina locales. Although the lush forest is not discernible on screen there are pivotal scenes shot in pools at the base of Bridal Veil Falls and Triple Falls. Asheville also picked up screen time in the mega-successful children-hunting-children franchise.

The quintessential North Carolina film, *Bull Durham*, takes place mostly in Durham, naturally. But Asheville plays a key cameo at the end of the movie. Kevin Costner's Crash Davis is released by the Bulls, still short of setting the all-time minor league home run record he has been chasing since the opening credits. He catches on with the Asheville Tourists and sets the record in Asheville with a homer into the trees beyond the left field fence. The scene was filmed in McCormick Field with a coach at the University of North Carolina-Asheville lofting fly balls hit with a fungo bat from shortstop.

The Biltmore Estate has been catnip to Hollywood directors since Van Heflin, Susan Haywood and Boris Karloff were tearing up the scenery in the Antebellum South potboiler *Tap Roots*, in 1948. America's largest private home has taken a star turn in more than a dozen films since, including *Being There*, *Richie Rich*, *Forrest Gump* and *Patch Adams*.

Hollywood has found other uses for the Asheville area as well through the years. Back during World War II days Aaron "Albert" Warner was plucked from a day job of handling financial matters for his family's famous movie studio, Warner Brothers, and put to work making propaganda films for the U.S. Army. "Major" Warner was also apparently an early "prepper" who was convinced the American coasts were under imminent attack. He had read in a military publication that Asheville and Hendersonville were among the "safe" places to reside and so he purchased the Crail Farm on Crab Creek Road in Henderson County.

The Major provisioned Crail Farm so well, including a herd of dairy cows, that it was said his family could live on the property "for an indefinite period" should the need arise. During his stay Warner hosted several of the studio's big name stars for vacations in his hideout. Crail Farm retained its Hollywood ties all the way until it was turned into the Crooked Creek Golf Club (the current clubhouse was stately Warner manor) in 1968. In the honorary foursome for the Grand Opening was none other than Jethro Bodine himself, Max Baer, Jr. of the hit television show, *The Beverly Hillbillies*. Baer was a crack golfer; a two-time Sacramento junior champion and the winner of that year's pro-am at the Andy Williams San Diego Open.

What's Up With...Balds?

When you move to Asheville you are going to find yourself on a hiking trail sooner than later. It is written in the rulebook that you must do so. And when you start hiking you are going to find that some of your best hikes are going to be on the nearby "balds" in the Blue Ridge Mountains. What are these things the local hikers are calling "balds?"

There are some things that science just can't explain. One of those is the presence of "balds" that are found only in the Southern Appalachian mountains. Balds are mountaintops that are covered only with dense swards of native grasses or blankets of evergreen shrubs - but no trees. Why some summits are bald and some are not is a total mystery. Clearing by indigenous peoples has been ruled out. So has predation by insects and lightning fires and unrelenting winds. Whatever their origins, these balds are here for Western North Carolinians to enjoy...

Black Balsam Knob. At 6,214 feet this grassy bald is the highest in the Blue Ridge. How good is the canine hiking here? There are some who will tell you the three miles of unobstructed views across Black Balsam Knob and neighboring Tennant Mountain comprise the best hike they have ever taken. And that may not even be the best hike at Black Balsam. The quickest way to the summit is on the *Art Loeb Trail* from where it crosses the access road (no trailhead signage but the line of cars will define it). After a scenic ten-minute climb in the thick balsam firs you are in the wide open expanses with views of the Blue Ridge Mountains in every direction for the next hour. You can close your loop with the *Investor Gap Trail*; backpackers can continue on to Cold Mountain of literary and

Looking out across the Sam Knob "bald."

Hollywood fame that you admire in the distance to the north. Matching hiking on Black Balsam Knob stride for stride in "wow" moments is the moderate climb to the Sam Knob summit on the opposite side of the trailhead lot. Sam Knob is another bald, albeit with clumps of shrubs so you will need to shift around the mountaintop to soak in the 360-degree views.

Max Patch Mountain. Deep in the bowels of the U.S. Forest Service's Harmon's Den area northwest of Asheville is Max Patch, the southernmost bald on the *Appalachian Trail*. It is named for the farmer who grazed cattle here back in the 1800s. But hey, Max Patch is not a natural bald - the Forest Service keeps the peak grassy with tractors. But this crown jewel of the Blue Ridge with its hiking loops across and around the 4,629-foot summit is so popular among Western North Carolinians that we can forgive its man-made assistance to bald status.

You can look for trees in every direction on the summit of Max Patch and not find any.

Roan Mountain. Roan Mountain, on the Tennessee-North Carolina border, is a treasure of the Blue Ridge Mountains. Dressed in a dark green spruce-fir forest and including the world's largest natural rhododendron garden, the Roan Mountain Highlands also sport the longest stretch of grassy bald in the Appalachian range. Roan Mountain is not actually a peak but a high ridge that runs five miles from a low point of 5,500 feet at Carver's Gap to 6,285 feet at Roan High Knob. The knob is accessed from a moderate 1.2-mile canine hike along the *Cloudland Trail*. In mid-June the hundreds of acres of Catawba rhododendrons erupt into a magenta riot, luring thousands of visitors to the mountain-top to travel through the canyons of blooms on a paved trail. As remarkable as Roan Mountain is, the opposite side of Carver's Gap shines even brighter as the *Appalachian Trail* crosses over three grassy balds in less than two hours of hiking. The third, Grassy Ridge Bald, rises to an elevation of 6,189 feet, making it the second highest grassy bald in the Appalachian Mountains. In fact, this is the only stretch of the *Appalachian Trail* that rises above 6,000 feet between Old Black 150 miles to the south and Mount Washington in New Hampshire, 1,500 miles to the north. The views, of course, are stunning.

Roan Mountain is a classic Southern Appalachian bald.

What's Up With...
Asheville's Unique Architecture?

There are two main reasons why your new hometown of Asheville has more Art Deco architecture than any town in the Southeast outside of Miami Beach - the talents of Douglas Ellington that got many landmark structures started and a crushing municipal debt that prevented future developers from tearing them down. Let's start with Ellington.

Douglas Ellington was born on the family farm in central North Carolina in 1886. His drawing talents took him to school at Randolph-Macon College in Lynchburg, Virginia, to Drexel Institute at the University of Pennsylvania in Philadelphia and finally to the prestigious Ecole des Beaux Arts in Paris, France where he became the first American to win the Prix de Rougevin. Ellington was well into his thirties

Douglas Ellington's landmark design for the Asheville City Hall.

when he returned to the United States.

He hung out his architectural shingle in Pittsburgh, Pennsylvania in 1920 with his brother running the business end of the practice. At about the same time Asheville was embarking on a building boom. Speculators who had grown rich on the Florida land frenzy of the early 1900s were looking for a place to spread their cash around and Western North Carolina got a large chunk of that money. There would be over 60 buildings constructed in downtown Asheville in the 1920s and Ellington picked up his first commission in the city in 1926, for the congregation of the First Baptist Church.

Ellington had worked in camouflage during World War I but his buildings did anything but blend into the surrounding streetscape. He favored the emerging Art Deco style with eye-catching colors, geometric patterns and flamboyant ornamentation. The First Baptist Church at Oak and Woodfin streets boasts polychromatic bricks set in an array of patterns and a two-story domed roof. Next up was Asheville City Hall that Ellington declared, "was an evolution of the desire that the contours of the building should reflect the mountain background." Ellington chose building materials that presented a "transition in color paralleling the natural clay-pink shades of the local Asheville soil." The eight-story iconic tower culminates in a Native American feather motif at the top.

Ellington continued on with designs for the Lewis Memorial Park Cemetery Office, the Merrimon Avenue Fire Station, the Biltmore

The Neo-Georgian Battery Park Hotel designed by William Stoddart was emblematic of the building boom in Asheville in the 1920s.

Ellington's design of the S&W Cafeteria on Patton Avenue is much admired.

Hospital and a monumental work for Asheville High School. Perhaps his finest work was slotted into the middle of Patton Avenue where Frank Sherrill and Fred Webber served up the first cafeteria-style food in North Carolina. For the S&W Cafeteria Ellington blended colorful repeating geometric designs of cream, green, blue, black and gilt glazed tiles into an Italian Renaissance design. At 583 Chunns Cove Road he constructed an eclectic summer house for himself using stone and bricks to add onto a century-old log cabin. Unlike most architects, Ellington was known to roll up his sleeves and get involved in the construction of the buildings he designed.

Then the Great Depression hit. In 1930 the City of Asheville was plunged into immediate debt - said to be $54 million, the largest per capita hole in the United States. Rather than declare bankruptcy city officials pledged the return of every dime it owed. For four decades there was no new construction in Asheville and when other municipalities became wrecking ball-crazed in the 1960s and 1970s there was no money in the Asheville coffers for urban renewal. Finally, the last obligation was paid in 1976 and the last bond was burned in front of Ellington's City Hall. By that time preservationist voices rang louder than renewal advocates and most of Asheville's unique streetscape survived.

Then there is Montford. Montford - no one knows where the name came from - emerged in 1890 when the Asheville Loan, Construction and Improvement Company announced plans to start selling building lots north of town. Asheville was in the early stages of its first growth spurt that would see the population rise from 2,500 in 1880 to over 50,000 before the onset of the Great Depression in 1930. Montford spread out across 300 acres and by 1893 there were 50 or so people here when the community incorporated as a town. The heady days of independence lasted until 1905 when Montford was swallowed by Asheville and became a city district on the north edge of downtown.

Richard Sharp Smith's interpretation of an old English field house for the 1900 Inn on Montford is representative of the architectural styles found in Montford.

Businessmen and lawyers and doctors moved into Montford - not the ultra-rich but well off enough for homeowners to mimic the popular building styles of the day and for some to hire architects. Most of the homes in Montford were constructed between 1890 and 1920. The earlier homes reflect the late Victorian era with Queen Anne and Shingle Style designs and later structures embraced the Arts and Crafts, Neoclassical and Colonial Revival trends that followed.

Montford went into a period of decline in the middle 1900s and bulldozers became an increasingly common sight on the curving, shaded streets. In December 1980, the Asheville City Council designated the Montford Historic District as the city's first local historic district. There are now four and Montford is the largest, as well as one of the largest in the state of North Carolina. More than 600 century-old structures are now protected.

What's Up With...the Drum Circle?

You may find folks around Asheville who remember Pritchard Park as the place their family went to pick up the mail - the city's main post office was in the three-story Federal Building that stood for 40 years on this wedge of land where several streets converge. Many more will remember the space as a place where they once caught the bus.

The current appearance of Pritchard Park dates to the early 2000s when it picked up a complete facelift from the city. One of the first groups attracted to Pritchard's new amphitheater under the sugar maples and ornamental cherry tress was Asheville's drumming community. On Friday evenings a dozen or so of the city's drummers would gather in the park to play traditional rhythms and trade off solos.

It did not take long for the informal drum circle to grow in popularity. The crowds and "noise" in the center of the city became an irritant to some but an agreement was hashed out that formally turned over Pritchard Park to the Asheville Drum Circle for free on Friday nights until 10:00 p.m.

The Asheville Drum Circle assembles on a Friday evening.

Over the years the years the drum circle has morphed away from ensemble recital to a celebration of drumming and dancing with 50 or more participants playing bongos, congas, dunduns, cowbells and more. There are no leaders and everyone is free to jump into the circle at any time.

The Friday night Asheville Drum Circle has come to symbolize the diversity of the city. That's a fine how-do-you-do to park namesake Jeter Connelly Pritchard. Pritchard was born in Tennessee in 1857 but came to North Carolina to run the *Roan Mountain Republican* newspaper. He became a lawyer in Madison County at the age of 20 when all you had to do was read for the law and pass the bar. Pritchard quickly segued into politics and in the 1890s became the first Republican elected to the United States Senate in the South since the days of Reconstruction twenty years earlier.

At the time, the black vote in America went almost exclusively to the Republicans - the party of Abraham Lincoln. Meanwhile many African-Americans were moving north to seek out factory jobs. With the number of eligible black votes shrinking in the South the Republican party split into the two factions: the traditional wing and the "lily white" wing which sought to drive all blacks from the party in order to chase votes going to the Democrats.

Leading the fight for the Lily-Whites in North Carolina was Jeter Pritchard. He opposed black officeholders in the state and worked to replace African-Americans in appointed positions with whites. Pritchard was appointed a federal judge by Theodore Roosevelt in 1904 and by the time he died in Asheville in 1921 at the age of 63 his vision had come to pass - almost all the black vote went to the Democrats.

The diversity of the Asheville Drum Circle would surprise Jeter Connelly Pritchard in his namesake park.

What's Up With... the Gee Haw Whimmy Diddle?

In Tennessee it is called a ziggerboo. In Georgia it is called a gee-haw. In Ohio it is called a lie detector. The Cherokees called it a voo-doo stick. In Western North Carolina it is called a whimmy diddle.

It is a classic Appalachian wooden folk toy, fashioned from small sticks, stripped of bark. One stick is carved with a series of notches on one end and a small propellor is attached to the notched end with a tiny brad or pin nailed into the end of the stick. Another stick is employed as a rubbing instrument which creates vibrations that set the propellor to spinning when rubbed across the notches. A deft practitioner can make the spinner turn right (gee, the command yelled by farmers to direct mules in the field) and left (haw) by imperceptibly switching the side the notches are stroked.

The best gee haw whimmy diddlers can make the kinetic toys dance back and forth dozens of times in just a few seconds. These masters have been gathering for the Annual World Gee Haw Whimmy Diddle Competition since the early 1980s. Some set their sights on besting the record of 56 back-and-forth rotations in 12 seconds while others look to entertain with hand switching and behind-the-back operations. Those who have won a competition before vie in a professional level; other categories are open to anyone. The battle for the title of world's best gee haw whimmy diddler is the centerpiece of the two-day Heritage Weekend in September put on by the Southern Highland Craft Guild at the Folk Art Center on the Blue Ridge Parkway.

The classic Appalachian folk toy - the gee haw whimmy diddle.

Living in Asheville

Celebrating around Asheville...

Once you move to the mountains of Western North Carolina you will need an extra calendar for the refrigerator to keep track of all the festivals. Here are some in Asheville that are especially anticipated...

River Arts District Studio Stroll
Spring Stroll in May, Fall Stroll in November

When the Southern Railway rolled into Asheville in the late 1800s to open up the town to outsiders this is where it came, hard by the east side of the French Broad River. Here the bottomland was wide and inviting before ascending to the city proper. The city's industry grew up around the railroad complex - the American Feed Milling Company, the Carolina Coal & Ice Company, the Asheville Cotton Mill, the Earle-Chesterfield Mill, the Standard Oil Distribution complex, the National Biscuit Company and dozens more.

Beginning with the Great Depression the manufacturing companies began closing or moving away. In 1985 artists started to filter into the abandoned industrial spaces and the first Studio Stroll was organized in 1994. There were 14 artists in the River Arts District (RAD). Today there are 200, give or take a ceramics artist or landscape painter or two. Most of the buildings are owned by artists. Their studios and galleries are tucked into 22 former factories and warehouses and you can visit any time and chance to find some at work and their doors open. But on two Studio Stroll weekends a year almost are in residence and free trolleys shuttle guests back and forth across the entire RAD.

The River Arts District is the largest artist-owned studio complex in the country.

Craft Fair of the Southern Highlands
July and October

The River Arts District shines with the talent of Asheville's local art community but the Southern Highland Craft Guild, headquartered at Milepost 382 on the Blue Ridge Parkway in Asheville, highlights the work of mountain artists from Alabama, Georgia, Kentucky, Maryland, the Carolinas, Tennessee, West Virginia, and Virginia. Since 1948 Guild members have staged expositions of their work.

These are juried shows for the craftspeople working in clay, metal, wood, jewelry, fiber, paper, natural materials, leather and mixed media. More than 200 make the grade and fill two floors of exhibition space in the U.S. Cellular Center for three days twice a year. At the Craft Fair of the Southern Highlands you can be sure that every exhibitor is the artist.

The Craft Fair of the Southern Highlands is the crafters' Super Bowl.

Asheville Wine and Food Festival
August

Asheville has a name for its food scene. They call it Foodtopia. And on one weekend every summer you can experience the full breadth of the city's gustatory wonders. The Asheville Wine and Food Festival only started in 2007 but it has already filled its plate with gushing accolades from the tourism press. Foodies can purchase a Grand Ticket (they usually go fast) and forage through scores of offerings from Asheville's top culinary artists and farm-to-table restaurants. For those with the chops, a Full Weekend Pass allows eaters to sample all the handcrafted artisanal foods and beverages. Single day options are also available and Saturday's ticket includes the not-to-be-missed Sweet & Savory's dessert creations.

Riverfest
August

Asheville's liveliest celebration of the French Broad River is Riverfest, the summer fundraiser for RiverLink, the watchdogs that look after the city's recreational water treasures. The festival on shore at the Salvage Station on Riverside Drive serves up food and beer and live music but the real treat comes out on the water as the Anything That Floats Parade drifts past. Entrants build their rafts or flotillas to compete for the coveted prizes of Most Creative, Green Machine (recycled materials), Funniest and Best Overall. Don't set sail without your costume.

National Gingerbread House Competition
November

Food historians tell us that gingerbread was first baked a thousand years ago. Medieval European bakers became so adept at creating complicated art forms out of gingerbread that only master bakers were permitted to bake gingerbread outside of Christmas and Easter. The origins of decorated gingerbread houses can be traced back to Germany in the early 1800s and attempts to re-create fairy-tale houses found in the stories by the brothers Grimm.

German emigrants brought the gingerbread house with them to America where it has become a Christmas architectural tradition. The National Gingerbread House Competition takes place each year at the Grove Park Inn, the Arts and Crafts marvel that just so happens to resembles a gingerbread house come to life. Constructors compete in four age categories for cash prizes and stays at the lodge.

All houses must rise on a two-foot square base and be constructed wholly of edible materials. The main structure must use at least 75% gingerbread and it should remain at least partially exposed. Judging takes place in November and entries are placed on display throughout the hotel until after the New Year.

Bele Chere RIP

There are times that Asheville likes to party a bit TOO much. Bele Chere began as a merchant-inspired outdoor street festival to revive the downtown business district in 1979. There was live music and local art and mountain food - all in a three-block area. After 35 years Bele Chere had grown

The tastiest architecture in Asheville shows up every year at the National Gingerbread House Competition.

into the largest free street festival in the entire Southeast, with more than a quarter-million people packing the streets of downtown Asheville. It was so big and so many streets had to be blocked off that the Bele Chere Frankenstein monster was actually hurting the downtown businesses that created it. A victim of its own success, Bele Chere was discontinued after 2013 - but keep an eye on your festival calendar in case the well-remembered celebration ever returns.

Cheering around Asheville...

Professional baseball came early to Asheville. The year was 1897 and there wasn't even an American League yet. But the population had tripled to more than 10,000 during the decade and Asheville was North Carolina's third largest city. The Asheville Moonshiners took the field in the Southeastern League, outfitted in uniforms provided by local hotelier Frank Loughran. Games were played at Allandale Park along the French Broad River and skipper John A. Jobe guided the Moonshiners to a respectable 11-10 record. But other teams in the league, which included the Atlanta Crackers and Columbus Babies, decided it took too darn long and too much money to take the train to the Western North Carolina mountains and booted the Moonshiners out of the league.

Asheville's baseball history resumed in 1910 and in 1915 the Moonshiners changed their name to the Tourists, launching one of minor league baseball's most enduring nicknames. A year earlier Asheville had gotten its first "real" ballyard with wooden grandstands in Oates Park, built at the corner of Southside Avenue and Choctaw Street. Olympic hero Jim Thorpe, recently signed by the New York Giants, cracked a three-run homer to beat the Asheville nine in an exhibition game in the park.

Asheville was also an early player in Negro League baseball, thanks to the efforts of Edward W. Pearson. Pearson came to Asheville in 1906 at the age of 34 after stints as a Buffalo Soldier in the Army's Ninth Calvary Division and the Chicago School of Law. He became a grocery store owner, developer, and promoter in West Asheville. The Buncombe County District Colored Agricultural Fair Pearson started in 1914 lasted for 33 years and he organized the first NAACP chapter in the state of North Carolina. In 1916 Pearson founded the Asheville Royal Giants and built Pearson Park in the Southside district for their games. Eventually Oates Park became the Royal Giants' primary home as the Tourists disbanded during World War I.

The year 1924 is a hallowed date in Asheville baseball lore. That was when the City of Asheville ponied up money to build a municipally

Baseball immortal Ty Cobb hit a home run in the first game at McCormick Field.

owned athletic park for the first time. Some $30,000 was used to buy up 15 acres off Biltmore Avenue and another $18,000 was used to construct the grandstand. The new pride of Asheville was not named for a local sports hero but for the city bacteriologist - Louis M. McCormick. Like so many others, McCormick was a transplant. After the 42-year old scientist arrived in 1905 he embarked on the nation's first research-based crusade against the common housefly. McCormick urged ordinances for cleaning livery stables and regulating garbage dumps. He called his campaign Swat That Fly! and encouraged children to knock on doors and offer to kill all houseflies for a dime. The program was initially mocked but by the time of his death from a heart condition in 1922, McCormick's Asheville model was adopted across the country.

To christen their new park the Tourists thought they would try a new name - the Skylanders. It didn't take and they were the Tourists again by Opening Day of the 1924 season. But the Skylanders lasted long enough to win the inaugural game in McCormick Field on April 3, 18-14 against the Detroit Tigers led by all-time great Ty Cobb. The Tigers belted four home runs in the exhibition, including one by Cobb. Lou Gehrig and Babe Ruth would also swat home runs in later exhibition games at McCormick Field. Ruth, in fact, was rumored to

McCormick Field has hosted minor league baseball longer than any other stadium in the sport.

have died in Asheville after visiting McCormick Field in 1925. He was only sidelined by intestinal problems that became "the bellyache heard round the world." Lovingly attributed in the press as being caused by eating too many hot dogs, most historians today cite a bout of syphilis for The Bambino missing a chunk of the 1925 season.

There has been other unusual baseball history made in Asheville. On August 30, 1916 the fastest game in professional baseball history was played at Oates Park - 31 minutes. It was late in the season and both the Asheville Tourists and the Winston-Salem Twins were basement dwelling teams with trains to catch. Every batter from both teams swung at the first pitch - usually just a lob from the pitcher - and after hitting the ball just continued running the bases until being tagged out. Players ran on and off the field to their positions, often not waiting for the final

Babe Ruth was rumored to have died after playing a baseball game in Asheville in 1925.

out of an inning to be recorded. The game also started one-half hour early and the first three innings were played without an umpire who was expecting the game to begin at its scheduled time. The Twins won 2-1 since they belted two home runs to Asheville's one. One person who was kept on his toes during the game was 15-year old Thomas Wolfe, who was said to have been the team's bat boy at the time.

On the final day of May in 1937 Asheville infielder Lynn Myers enjoyed a game at McCormick Field unlike any other in professional baseball. Richmond pitcher Bill Yarewick was wild that day - he would walk 18 Tourists batsmen. Myers drew five walks and was hit twice by a pitch. He scored every time he reached base in the 30-3 Asheville rout. Seven runs scored without an official plate appearance. That is one for the record books.

Although McCormick Field is exclusively a baseball field as it approaches its second century it has hosted other sporting events in the past. The Asheville High School Cougars played both their baseball and football games here until 1948. When the Tourists were on a brief hiatus in the late 1950s a tight quarter-mile asphalt track was installed for a transformation into the McCormick Field Speedway. Included in the weekly stock car events was one Grand National stock car race with short track specialist Jim Paschal taking the checkered flag.

By 1990 McCormick Field was the oldest active ballpark in the minor leagues. It was decided to spend $3 million to bring down the old wooden grandstands - a fire waiting to happen - and replace them with concrete while retaining the same layout. The orientation of the field, with its famous short porch to the trees in right field, would also stay the same. The ridged-tin wall in right would go from 12 feet high to 36 feet, however. It is even higher in right center field; at 42 feet no wall in professional baseball is higher than McCormick Field.

For much of its history Asheville's minor league franchise was only two jumps from the major leagues. Local fans got to see such future Hall-of-Famers as Craig Biggio and Eddie Murray and Willie Stargell, who was known as "On the Hill Will" in Asheville for the home runs he sent sailing over that right field fence only 297 feet from home plate. Since the Colorado Rockies formed in 1993 Asheville has been their farm team in the South Atlantic League, one of the longest major

Doggies at the Diamond is one of the many promotional nights held by the Asheville Tourists at McCormick Field.

league-minor league affiliations in baseball. The "Sally League" is one of the lowest levels in the minor league ball and today's players are many rungs from stardom in the Show.

But that doesn't deter the Asheville Tourists from setting new attendance records each season. McCormick Field is especially popular on Thirsty Thursdays, when beer is dispensed for a dollar. Tourists' general manager Ron McKee introduced in the promotion in 1983 and trademarked the term a dozen years later as it became a staple in minor league parks across America. Every time that promotion is run it must be accompanied by a letter of written permission from the Asheville Tourists.

In basketball, March Madness did not begin in Asheville but the Southern Conference was the first to stage a post-season tournament, back in 1921. That first tournament was played in Atlanta and won by the University of North Carolina that competed in the Southern Conference until 1953. In the 1980s the Southern Conference men's basketball tournament landed in the Asheville Civic Center and stayed for a dozen years. The hoopsters have been back since 2012 for the chance to compete in the NCAA Men's Division I Basketball Tournament. The local favorite is Western Carolina University from Cullowhee which has won one league championship - in 1996.

Dogwalking around Asheville...

One of the many "Best Places" lists that Asheville often graces is pet-friendliest. In fact, it seems as if pet ownership is a requirement for residency in the Land of the Sky. So where are some of the best places those dogs are taking their owners in Asheville?

Azalea Park (Azalea Road, off Swannanoa Road, NC 81). This Asheville greenspace, while primarily a paradise for soccer players, nonetheless serves up a smorgasbord of delights for your dog in small doses. Beyond the fields, short, rutted jeep trails lead to the shallow Swannanoa River that flows in a series of low dams and pools for some superb doggie paddling. For a little cardio there is a gated road opposite that open field which leads up a wooded hillside. And for some socializing there is a fenced-in dog park a little further down Azalea Road.

Bent Creek Experimental Forest (off Brevard Road, NC 191). After the National Forest Service purchased this land it set aside 1,100 acres around Bent Creek for research by the Appalachian Forest Experiment Station, which Congress had established in 1921 as one of the oldest experimental forests in the East. There are no great destinations in Bent Creek Forest, no spectacular waterfalls, no awe-inspiring views. What there is, however, is great woods-walking with your dog on gated jeep roads and foot trails that ease you up the slopes on long, sinuous hikes. Bent Creek and its 44 miles of trails is not the place to come for a quick leg-stretcher. Your dog will find the easiest trotting around 13-acre Lake Powhatan, formed when the creek was dammed in 1942. You will find plenty of company on the trails as well.

These verdant stream-bottom communities are thick with rhododendron and stands of white pine and hemlock which thin out the further you venture up the slopes. One of the best hiking loops with your dog without driving too deep into the forest is up the *Ledyard* and *Wolf* branches north of Lake Powhatan. In the course of almost five miles you pass through fern-encrusted clearcuts, regenerating hardwood forests and selected harvest plots.

Bent Creek abounds with roomy forest service roads.

French Broad River Park (Amboy Road from Exit 1C off I-240). Public recreation first came to the banks of the French Broad River in Asheville in 1904 when the Asheville Electric Company built Riverside Park and transported folks out on their trolleys to enjoy the carousel and walking paths. Movies were shown on the banks of the river that could only be viewed by boat. Riverside Park was crippled by a fire in 1915 and completely destroyed by flooding a year later.

In the 1990s development began again with French Broad River Park which won a Heritage Park Award as one of the 10 best parks in America funded with a land and water conservation fund grant. The French Broad River Greenway links French Broad River Park and Carrier Park with an hour of canine hiking along a paved, level path tracing the water's edge. Anchoring the corridor in French Broad River Park is a two-section dog park - behind the dog park is your dog's best access from the high banks for a swim.

Mountains-to-Sea Trail (Blue Ridge Parkway). Conceived in the 1970s by Howard Lee, then Secretary of the North Carolina Department of Natural Resources and Community Development, a coalition of public agencies and private volunteers are attempting to cobble together a hiking path of over 930 miles from Clingman's Dome in the Great Smoky Mountains to Jockey's Ridge on Cape Hatteras, the highest sand dune on the Atlantic Coast. In 1982, a 75.8-mile trail along the Cape Hatteras National Seashore became the first segment of the trail to be dedicated. To date a little more than 500 somewhat disjointed miles of the *Mountains-to-Sea Trail* (MST) have been completed, mostly in the mountains and at the sea. The MST tags the Blue Ridge Parkway for about 300 of its miles and around Asheville the 60 miles of the MST between Mount Mitchell and Mount Pisgah are maintained by the Carolina Mountain Club. This stretch was designated a National Recreation Trail in 2005.

The Mountains-to-Sea Trail snakes it way along the Blue Ridge Parkway.

The MST hops back and forth across the Blue Ridge Parkway and 30 trail segments have been identified. One of the most convenient places to sample the trail from Asheville is at the Parkway Visitor Center (where a descriptive brochure identifies the 30 trailheads) at Milepost 384.4. The MST is across the Parkway from the Visitor Center and a 1.2-mile loop has been created (one of the crossings is under the Parkway through a stone-faced tunnel). The easy going here is a superb introduction to the trail for the novice canine hiker.

North Carolina Arboretum (NC 191 Exit from the Blue Ridge Parkway at Milepost 393). Frederick Law Olmsted is recognized as the founder of American landscape architecture and the nation's foremost parkmaker. Olmsted's genius shaped the cities of New York, (Central Park), Boston (Emerald Necklace), and Montreal (Mount Royal Park) among scores of others. His last major project was George William Vanderbilt's Biltmore Estate (a splendid place to hike with your dog as well but admission is required), which Olmsted laid out while in his seventies. He died before his dream of establishing an arboretum on the grounds could be realized. Olmsted's vision did not begin taking shape until the 1980s when 426 acres in the Pisgah National Forest were allocated for a true plant museum. In the 1990s the first gardens dedicated to the Southern Appalachian region were installed.

You aren't likely to take a prettier hike with your dog in the Blue Ridge than in the North Carolina Arboretum, whether it be through wildflowers or planted gardens. Eventually the groomed woodland paths will land canine hikers on the Bent Creek Road, a wide, flat multi-purpose artery that hugs the gentle meanderings of Bent Creek. If the traffic is heavy you can lead your dog onto the dirt footpaths that occasionally slip between the road and the creek. Not to be missed is the maze of short paths that wander through the National Native Azalea Collection that decorate the floodplain from March to August with 16 of the 17 azalea species native to the United States. All of the canine hiking around Bent Creek is easy going. If you are hiking into the Arboretum from Lake Powhatan Recreation Area, this is the road/trail you are on when you go through the chain link gate.

Your dog won't be in a hurry to race through the trails of the North Carolina Arboretum.

For dogs looking for a sportier hiking day in the

North Carolina Arboretum depart Bent Creek and climb the Rocky Cove Road or Hard Times Road which are linked by the one-mile, pine-scented *Owl Ridge Trail* to form a splendid loop. The roads link outside the gates in Pisgah National Forest for an even more challenging canine hike.

Richmond Hill Park (Richmond Hill Drive off Pearson Bridge Road from Riverside Drive). Richmond Pearson, United States Congressman and diplomat, was born on January 26, 1852 in Yadkin County, the fourth of five children of Richmond Pearson, Chief Justice of the North Carolina Supreme Court; both his grandfathers were United States senators. The family land here covered 820 acres, upon which Pearson constructed a grand mansion in 1889, considered one of the most elegant and innovative buildings of its time. Plans were drawn up by James G. Hill, a one-time Supervising Architect for the United States Treasury. Today, 183 acres of the former Pearson estate is preserved as Richmond Hill Park, Asheville's largest city park.

Hiking with your dog along the Richmond Hill trail system is akin to moving around a giant model railroad layout. Trail sections pass next to one another and intersect often - there are three sets of blazes and you will see yellow and blue and red blazes throughout your dog's journey here. The marquee canine hike on Richmond Hill is the *Yellow Loop* that motors up and down the slopes, sweeps by the French Broad River three times and makes several stream crossings. Encased completely in a mixed-hardwood forest on paw-friendly footpaths, this is a thoroughly enjoyable 2.75-mile ramble for your dog. The red blazes all leave and come back to the *Yellow Loop* which will add spice to your dog's Richmond Hill experience when you return. The trail system, designed by the Southern Off-Road Bicycle Association, sports its share of tight turns and ups and downs as your dog trots along.

Warren Wilson College Trails (Swannanoa, Exit 55 off I-40). Warren Wilson College began life in 1894 as the Asheville Farm School with 25 boys attending the first three grades of elementary instruction, guided by the Women's Board of Home Missions of the Presbyterian Church. Over the decades it evolved into a secondary school, acquiring the name of a church official, and emerged in 1972 as a four year-college. Today, in addition to their classwork, students are required to perform at least 100 hours of community service and work on-campus for the institution which operates a 300-acre working farm and maintains a 600-acre forest boasting 25 miles of hiking trails, most of which, save for the *Suicide Ridge Trails*, are open to the public.

The star walk on the college grounds is the *River Trail* which, if your dog loves to swim, will be the longest two-mile hike you ever take. The easy-going waters of the Swannanoa River are a perfect complement for the pace of your stroll along the flat dirt path. There are deep pools and riffles the entire way but the best doggie swimming hole comes at the beaches when the river starts a 180-degree turn. The trail doesn't leave the water until the last half-mile where it joins up with the *Dam Pasture Trail* and carries another mile to a parking area if you have a car shuttle. Otherwise it is back the way you came for more swimming and close up views of the Warren Wilson farm where your dog can channel his inner cattle dog.

For a stiffer test for your dog there are the *Dam Pasture Trails* and the *Jones Mountain Trails*, both of which make ample use of old farm roads on exceedingly paw-friendly paths. There is only a brief visit to Bull Creek under the pines in Dam Pasture and no water at all on the climb to 2,753-foot Jones Mountain (winter views only at the summit) so your dog may demand a return trip to the *River Trail* before you leave campus.

It doesn't get any better than the Swannanoa River for your water-loving dog.

Drinking around Asheville...

In the full sweep of history for the world's oldest and most widely consumed alcoholic drink, Asheville might be the last city expected to shoulder the mantle of Beer City USA. Heck, when the 18th Amendment in 1920 made Prohibition the law of the land that was already the fourth time alcohol had been banned in Asheville.

At that time there had been no legal drinking in North Carolina anyway since 1908. Asheville had been the first town to vote for the state-wide prohibition of alcohol. The impetus to shut down "Hell's Half Acre," a swath of downtown that supported 18 saloons, was a murderous rampage by a chain gang escapee named Will Harris. Harris gunned down five men, including two peace officers, in the streets of Asheville in November of 1906, fueled by a quart of bourbon. Harris was tracked down the next day in Fletcher by a posse that riddled his body with over 100 bullets.

After the 18th Amendment was repealed in 1933 Asheville did not take to the streets with beer mugs raised in triumph. The North Carolina ban on alcohol lasted two more years. By that time the liquor of choice was moonshine, whose popularity soared during Prohibition since it was the easiest alcohol to obtain.

These Prohibition-era officials would no doubt disapprove of today's Beer City USA.

It would be 50 more years before Uli Bennewitz, a Bavarian immigrant who came to the Outer Banks as an agricultural consultant for a 9,000-acre farm, started the state's first brewpub. Being Bavarian, it never occurred to Bennewitz that beer-making was illegal in North

Carolina and that Dare County where he was operating was dry. But being an agricultural consultant, Bennewitz pressed his case that brewing is a benefit to the state's farmers and a North Carolina brewpub law was passed in 1986. Bennewitz called North Carolina's first brewpub the Weeping Radish for the large tubers that often complement a good Bavarian beer - all his brews comply with the Bavarian Reinheitsgebot Purity Law of 1516 after all.

A common sight in Beer City USA.

In 1994 Oscar Wong, a retired engineer, and his partner John McDermott brought micro brewing to Asheville. At the time the city had no beer scene. It had, really, no scene at all. Many of the buildings downtown were abandoned and covered by plywood panels. Wong set up his Highland Brewing Company operation in a musty cellar beneath Barley's Tap Room on Biltmore Avenue. It was the fourth craft brewery in North Carolina. Wong set the model for the city's future craft brewers early on when he sent 375 pints of Asheville's first legal beer down the drain because, while drinkable, the batch did not meet his standards.

Two years later the Great Smokies Craft Brewers Invitational was born in Asheville, with maybe 300 tickets sold. More than twenty years later that event is known as Brewgrass and there are probably that many people on the grounds just working for the 50+ breweries represented. There are more than two dozen brewpubs in Asheville, enough to give the city 8.8 breweries per 100,000 people in the metro area. Only residents in Boulder and Fort Collins in Colorado and Bend in Oregon have better access to handcrafted suds. No wonder the city is well on its way to completing a six-pack of Beer City USA titles.

Driving around Asheville...

Asheville owes its existence to the Buncombe Turnpike, a 75-mile road carved out of the 1820s wilderness from the South Carolina border to the Tennessee border that opened up the North Carolina mountains to settlement for the first time. Three Asheville men were authorized to bankroll the project so you have a good idea where the route was going to go. One of the trio was James Washington Patton who also built an east-west road to service his Eagle Hotel - Patton Avenue is still the main crosstown thoroughfare in downtown Asheville.

A century later another road was planned through the Blue Ridge Mountains and designers routed it down the Unaka Mountains in Tennessee towards the Great Smoky Mountains National Park. When civic leaders in Asheville got wind of the routing they sprang into action. By the time the Asheville boosters were finished in Washington the Blue Ridge Parkway was headed for the Land of The Sky when ground was broken in 1935.

Tollbooths like this one were constructed on the Parkway in the 1950s but they were never authorized to collect fees. The Parkway remains free to use and the booths were removed in the 1980s after two were smashed by errant drivers.

Today the Blue Ridge Parkway's 459 miles of two-lane blacktop are the most popular destination in the National Park Service with some 19 million visitors each year. Many of Asheville's two million annual tourists disgorge from the Parkway. Locals use the Parkway as well, you will often see cars parked on the side of the road near Asheville at hiking spots not listed on the official brochure - the Shut-In Trail at Milepost 393, the Green Knob Lookout Tower at Milepost 350.4, Rattlesnake Lodge at Milepost

374.4 and Craven Gap at Milepost 377.4 among them.

The locals also have their own "best drives." They come with names like Devil's Whip, Tail of the Dragon, Diamondback, Cherohala Skyway and Moonshiner 28. The mountain roads around Asheville are so spectacular even Interstate 26 has been designated a state scenic byway, the only such stretch of interstate so honored in North Carolina.

No local drive was ever more beloved than the road to the top of Chimney Rock, now part of Chimney Rock State Park. In 1956, sports car enthusiasts began eyeing the serpentine road up the 315-foot landmark and soon the Chimney Rock Hillclimb competition was underway. Racing against the clock, tires squealing through 13 pigtail turns, the Hillclimb became a fixture on the Sports Car Club of America calendar until 1995.

Despite the fact that there was no money involved the Hillclimb attracted drivers from across the country, including a few big-name NASCAR drivers. All that was on the line was a silver trophy and the coveted title of that year's King of the Hill. By its later years the best would complete the hair-raising two-mile drive in under two minutes. Thousands of spectators would turn out for the Hillclimb and many would jump into the cars of their favorite drivers for an equally harrowing ride back down the hill.

Harry Ingle of Charlotte, piloting a Zink Super Vee, became the first Chimney Rock Hillclimb King of the Hill to complete the course in under two minutes in 1971. In 1973, Ingle was the Sports Car Club of America's Super Vee National Champion.

Eating around Asheville...

Philadelphia has its cheesesteaks. Maine has its lobsters. North Carolina has its barbecue. More ink - and vinegar - has been spilled on North Carolina barbecue and the best places to find it than all other culinary topics combined. After moving to Asheville you will either quickly discover your barbecue sweet spot or join the search for your favorite 'cue castle (and there are no barbecue joints in Buncombe County on the 24-stop North Carolina Barbecue Society Historic Barbecue Trail). There are only a couple of things you need to know first.

Over the decades two types of barbecue have evolved, not always cordially, across the Tar Heel State. In Eastern style "every part of the hog except the squeal" is slow-cooked; in Western style (also known as Lexington style) only the pork shoulder of the pig is used. Eastern style barbecue sauce is vinegar and red pepper-based; Western style barbecue includes ketchup or tomato products as a third main ingredient. You may also run into mustard-based sauce that sneaks up from South Carolina.

A proper Asheville barbecue meal features the mandatory sides of hushpuppies, cole slaw ("red slaw" tosses mayonnaise in favor of the Lexington-style barbecue sauce), and banana pudding. You traditionally wash it all down with sweet tea but if you are going all-in on North Carolina...Taste the Legend.

Over in New Bern, back in 1893, Caleb Davis Bradham's medical career was derailed by his father's failing business and so he returned to his hometown and opened the Bradham Drug Company store. Soon he was offering a new concoction, "Brad's Drink," at

Pepsi Cola was birthed in a corner drug store in New Bern, North Carolina.

his soda fountain which he believed helped ease digestion. By 1898 he was calling his blend of "carbonated water, sugar, pepsin, kola nut extract, vanilla and 'rare oils'" "Pepsi-Cola" and North Carolina's most famous soft drink was born. But not North Carolina's most beloved soda pop.

That would be Cheerwine. About the same time Pepsi-Cola was being mixed by hand in the back of Caleb Bradham's pharmacy Lewis D. Peeler, a general storekeeper in his mid-thirties in Salisbury, was getting interested in the new soft drink business. He began experimenting with flavors in the basement of his store on Council Street, near the railroad station. In 1913 Peeler bought a franchise from the Mint-Cola Bottling Company in Kentucky to manufacture its drink in North Carolina. When World I cut off critical supplies of sugar Mint-Cola went bankrupt and Peeler and some investors bought the assets to start the Carolina Beverage Company.

Peeler went searching for a carbonated beverage that wouldn't require so much sugar. He found the answer in 1917 when a flavor salesman from St. Louis came calling with a wild cherry flavor pulled from the oil of almond. The core extract was blended with 11 other flavors into the Mint Cola base, given extra carbonation and out came Cheerwine, so named for its rich burgundy hues. In 1926 Peeler trademarked the name and the following year he began bottling Cheerwine in Charlotte, where it is still created today.

The coming of the Internet helped leak out the secret of the "Nectar of North Carolina" and the soft drink has achieved something of cult status in recent years, even garnering a feature article in the *New York Times* in 2011. To help slake demand for its cherry soda sensation Carolina Beverage - the oldest soft drink company in America run by the same family - has created a Cheerwine finder on its website. Luckily for Western North Carolinians they can just stop into their local store to "Taste the Legend."

Snacking in North Carolina means boiled peanuts, obtained from roadside stands. Peanuts have been favorites in the Carolinas since they first arrived on slave ships in the 1700s. The legumes were pulled raw from the ground and boiled in salt water that delivered a distinctive twang. As peanuts became popular around the country the preparation of choice was roasting. Only a swath of North and South Carolina clung to the traditional boiled peanut. When a northern newspaper account in the 1920s tried to explain that the most popular seller at Southern fruit and peanut stands was the boiled peanut it added that most readers would not recognize a peanut boiling unless "you have visited the 'goober' sections of the Carolinas."

Coming soon to a roadside shack near you.

Listening around Asheville...

Appalachian music goes back as far as the first fiddles brought by Scotch Irish settlers to the Blue Ridge mountains in the 1700s. Banjoes brought to America by West African slaves were incorporated into the folk songs in the 1800s. By 1928, when local attorney and folklorist Bascom Lamar Lunsford lured front porch pickers from the hills and hollers to perform in public at the Asheville Chamber of Commerce's Rhododendron Festival, bluegrass music was entrenched in southern Appalachia.

That first festival was held on Pack Square and the music and dancing were so popular the Mountain Dance and Folk Festival became its own attraction. Quickly ensconced in the Asheville Civic Auditorium, the festival is still going strong after 90 years. Lunsford, known as the "Minstrel of the Appalachians," performed until suffering a stroke in

Bascom Lamar Lunsford hears an audition for an appearance at his Mountain Dance and Folk Festival.

1965, always appearing in a starched white shirt and black bow tie to remind the crowd that this was not stereotypical "hillbilly music."

Not much had changed in the Asheville music scene in 1978 when a 44-year old New York City engineer named Bob Moog moved to town for the mountains. His Moog synthesizer had helped remake electronic music over the previous decade. Moog had this to say about his new surroundings, "One doesn't hear much talk of synthesizers here in Western North Carolina. Most of the local musical instrument stores cater to fiddlers, pickers, and the disciples of Elvis the King." You can still see Moog instruments being crafted in Asheville at the Moog Factory at 160 Broadway.

It was the early 1990s when today's fabled Asheville music scene began to crystallize. Two legendary venues opened downtown, Vincent's Ear and Be Here Now. The latter began booking national acts which helped place out-of-the-way Asheville on the touring map. About the same time Asheville native Warren Haynes was building a following as a lead guitarist in a re-formed Allman Brothers Band and founder of his own southern rock jam band, Gov't Mule. Haynes launched a Christmas Jam in 1989 that has become an Asheville institution, attracting such players as Dave Matthews, Jackson Browne, Counting Crows, The Blind Boys of Alabama and many more.

Today in Asheville music fans can count on seeing a steady stream of national acts in addition to experiencing a vibrant local scene. The US Cellular Center, opened in 1974, can seat as many as 7,000 and its Thomas Wolfe Auditorium offers a more intimate setting with 2,500 seats. Among the city's many music venues the Grey Eagle is an important presenter of indie acts in an old warehouse and the Orange Peel has been name one of the Top 5 Rock Clubs in the Nation by *Rolling Stone* magazine. The Orange Peel operates out of the one-time Skateland Rollerdome and takes its name from a pioneering R & B Club from the 1960s.

But as good as the music is indoors in Asheville you can often find its equal on the downtown streets. Street performers, or buskers as they have been known since Queen Victoria days in Great Britain, have been woven into the fabric of downtown Asheville since the 1980s. The musicians and spoon players and human statues are on the job, working for tips. You may see some of the acts in clubs as well but for most this is how they earn their keep in Asheville. So drop a little something in the tip jar as you enjoy the show.

Any time the weather is warm and you come into downtown Asheville you will treated to a smorgasbord of traditional Americana played by a jug band on one corner, Dixieland jazz on another or violin-picking down the street. Busker code dictates that a performer should abandon a favorite pitch (performing spot) every two hours so there is a constant infusion of entertainment in the downtown Asheville street scene.

While buskers play a central role in forging Asheville's cultural identity, the performances are not reserved for tourists. Locals enjoy the intimate live performances of "Rocky Top" as well. The best places to catch busking are at the western end of Pack Square; on Haywood Street in front of Woolworth Walk, an old five-and-dime converted into gallery space; and at the Flat Iron Sculpture at the point of Wall Street and Battery Park Avenue.

Sometimes the best sounds in Asheville come from the street.

The Towns Around Town...

Biltmore Village

Cornelius Vanderbilt began his career working on his father's ferry in New York harbor in 1805. When he died in 1877 after a career in shipping and railroading the Commodore was the wealthiest man in America and the richest man ever to die. He had been a bit of a tightwad himself but his descendants knew how to spend money. After a trip to Western North Carolina in 1888, when he was 26 years old, grandson George William Vanderbilt decided to build a country home. He began buying land and didn't stop until he had 125,000 acres.

Vanderbilt hired Richard Morris Hunt to build his house. Hunt was the first American to be admitted to the École des Beaux-Arts in Paris – the finest school of architecture in the world - and he delivered a French Renaissance chateau just south of downtown Asheville. When the 250-room Biltmore was completed in 1895 it was, and remains, the largest privately owned home in the United States. Vanderbilt's only child, Cornelia Stuyvesant Vanderbilt, opened Biltmore House to the public in 1930; family members continued to live here until 1956,

Pebbledash construction was used to highlight Richard Morris Hunt's distinctive architectural vision for Biltmore Village.

when it was permanently opened to the public as a house museum.

Vanderbilt also created Biltmore Village as a place for his estate workers to live. Hunt and Frederick Law Olmsted, the "Father of American Landscape Architecture" and the co-creator of New York's Central Park, teamed up to create an English-style manor community on Biltmore's doorstep. Hunt's office was in the center of the village and the postcard-worthy All Souls church is the only one of the famous architect's six churches still extant. Asheville boasted one of the world's first electric street railways and Biltmore Village was its destination when it opened in 1889.

High Time To Visit

BILTMORE BLOOMS
STARTS FIRST DAY OF SPRING

Outside the exuberant castle is an 8,000-acre estate that includes a forest, a farm, a winery and gardens designed by Olmsted that were his last project. If you have ever wondered what 100,000 flowers in bloom look like, this is your chance - from daffodils and tulips in April to azaleas and snapdragons in May. The annual spring pilgrimage includes live music daily, winery tastings and an annual Easter Egg Hunt on the front lawn of Biltmore House.

Waynesville

The largest town in Western North Carolina west of Asheville was founded by Robert Love in 1810 who gave the land for the courthouse and downtown area. Love had served in the Revolutionary War as a young man and he renamed the then-Mount Prospect after his flamboyant commander, General "Mad" Anthony Wayne. Wayne was one of the most honored warriors for independence - 18 towns and cities were named for him as well as scores of boroughs, counties, schools and streets.

Waynesville is the anchor of Haywood County, resting in a valley a half-mile high among some of the tallest peaks in the Blue Ridge

Mountains. The downtown area is an art and shopping destination and a short drive away are the resort area of Maggie Valley, the Harrah's Cherokee Casino and the Great Smoky Mountains National Park.

High Time to Visit

Folkmoot
July

It was back in 1973 that Clinton Border traveled with a square dance team to a folk festival in England. After returning to Waynesville Border worked for the next decade to bring an international folk festival to Western North Carolina. Folkmoot, meaning a "meeting of the people," debuted in 1984. In the three decades since over 200 folk groups from more than 100 countries have made their way to Waynesville to put their cultural heritage on display with indigenous costumes, traditional music and native dances. In 2003 the ten-day Folkmoot was recognized by the North Carolina General Assembly as the state's official international folk festival.

Weaverville

The prominent stone obelisk on Pack Square in downtown Asheville is dedicated to Zebulon Baird Vance, a United States congressman and eloquent supporter of the Union until the very outbreak of the Civil War. Nevertheless, Vance chose loyalty to his home state once hostilities began. In Asheville, he organized the Confederate Rough and Ready Guards; as colonel of the 26th North Carolina Regiment, he gained such fame for his courage that he was elected governor of North Carolina in 1862 and again in 1864. Until his death in 1894 Vance spent most of his time either in the Governor's Mansion or his office in the United States Senate.

The Weaverville area, north of the city, is where Vance, known for his sharp and earthy wit, was born in 1830 in a log cabin in Reems Creek, the son of a farmer and country merchant. The Weavers, John and Elizabeth, were among the earliest settlers in these parts, back in the

The Howland trolley ferried passengers between Asheville and Weaverville.

1780s. The town proper did not get under way for another 100 years, on land donated by Michael Montraville Weaver in 1875. There were soon rambling resort hotels with names like Dula Springs and Blackberry Lodge where guests came to enjoy the clean air of Dry Ridge. In 1909 a private trolley was built from that obelisk on Pack Square the six miles to Weaverville. Rex Howland's trolley only lasted about a decade but visitors are still finding their way to the small mountain town.

High Time to Visit

WEAVERVILLE ART SAFARI
SPRING AND FALL

Twice a year - in spring and fall - Weaverville area artists open their studio doors and invite the public into their workspaces for the Art Safari. There are several such opportunities around Asheville for art enthusiasts: Kenilworth Art Studio Tour in May, Toe River Studio Tour in June, Leicester Studio Tour in August, Open Studio Tour of Henderson County in September, and the Haywood Art Studio Tour in October.

Black Mountain

Black Mountain, 13 miles east of Asheville, comes by its occasional nickname as "the Front Porch of Western North Carolina" honestly. In 1915 Mount Mitchell became North Carolina's first state park and one of the first in the Southeast. And Black Mountain was the jumping off point to reach the park. "The motor road to the top of the world," gushed promotional brochures. At 6,684 feet the peak is not quite that high but it is the tallest point in America east of the Rocky Mountains. Elisha Mitchell, a science professor at the University of North Carolina, fell from a cliff above a 40-foot waterfall and died trying to prove it in the 1850s.

In 1911 the Mount Mitchell Railroad left town from a spur of the Southern Railway on its 21-mile journey to Camp Alice, just one-half mile from the summit of Mount Mitchell. The quarry was spruce pine

When the automobile became popular so too did the drive up Mount Mitchell from Black Mountain.

and when it was all chopped down the owners converted the railroad bed into the "Mount Mitchell Motor Road," a cinder-surfaced, one-way toll road to the top of the mountain. Tourism was so popular that a second toll road was built up the east flank of the Black Mountains.

In 1933 educator John Andrew Rice gathered three fellow teachers and enrolled 21 students in Black Mountain College. He had a vision for an experimental school that would place the study and practice of the arts at the center of a liberal arts education. It would also be owned and operated by the faculty. Black Mountain College attracted some of the mid-20th century's most talented visual artists, composers and designers. The school only lasted until 1957 but a museum and art center in downtown Asheville preserves the legacy of the legendary school while the town itself remains a bastion for the arts.

High Time to Visit

Sourwood Festival
August

Since the 1970s the town has staged a street fair to celebrate the buttery taste of gourmet sourwood honey, culled from the summer-blooming flowers of the sourwood tree that is indigenous to the Southern Appalachians. Some 30,000 people turn out each year to browse more than 200 vendor tents and compare the current sourwood honey harvest.

Hendersonville

Leonard Henderson was a North Carolina lawyer of some repute who was named as one of the three justices to the first State Supreme Court in 1818. He was the Chief Justice when he died in 1833 at the age of 61. Henderson never had anything to do with Western North Carolina but he died at about the time the southern chunk of Buncombe County was becoming its own county. Not only was the new municipality named for Henderson in 1838 but he also got the county seat named for him in 1841, which seems overly generous.

Hendersonville evolved into the second city of the Carolina Blue Ridge, after Asheville. Hendersonville was "the dancingest town in America," a tradition that began with street dances to celebrate the end of World War I. Mostly that dancing meant clogging, the descendant of the fancy steps the Irish and Scotch settlers brought with them when they migrated to the Southern Appalachian mountains. When you go to downtown Hendersonville for the street dances in the summer you will be observed by a platoon of life-size, whimsically painted acrylic bears, another Hendersonville institution but one that dates only to 2003.

A sleuth of bears gather before fanning out to Hendersonville streets.

High Time to Visit

NORTH CAROLINA APPLE FESTIVAL
LABOR DAY

North Carolina apple growers tell us that America's favorite fruit is good for your teeth, stomach, complexion, nerves and overall good health. The warm days and cool nights of the Western North Carolina mountains are ideal for growing crisp, juicy apples. Henderson County grows 65 percent of the state's four million bushels of apples, the seventh biggest producing county in the United States.

The celebration of the region's signature crop takes place in Hendersonville for four days over Labor Day. While most North Carolina apples are of four varieties (Red Delicious, Golden Delicious, Rome Beauty and Gala) the star of the festival is usually the tasty Honeycrisp which is one of the earliest apples to market. The Apple Festival has been a tradition since the 1940s; highlights include a nine-block street fair and Labor Day parade. Make sure you keep at least one hand free to carry a half-peck bag home.

Brevard

Brevard is famous for so many things the town can't fit it all on one marquee. It is a mecca for mountain bikers as the gateway to Pisgah National Forest. It is the jumping off point for tours of Transylvania County's 250 waterfalls. Music lovers from around the country mark off their calendars each summer for the Brevard Music Center Festival which hosts 400 high school and college musicians, ages 14-29, from across the world who study and give over 80 public performances and attracts tens of thousands of listeners each year. The students reside on the 180 wooded acres nestled against the Blue Ridge Mountains. Keith Lockhart, Conductor of the Boston Pops Orchestra, has been the Artistic Director since 2007. The downtown shopping has attracted the attention of *USA Today* which called O.P. Taylor's one of the Top Ten toy stores in the world.

High Time to Visit

WHITE SQUIRREL FESTIVAL
Memorial Day

Where would science fiction writers be without the nefarious circus train crash to kickstart their hair-raising sagas? Madison, Florida suffered one of those dreaded circus transport incidents in 1949 when a carnival truck left the road and tipped over. But the consequences were not that scary. Some white squirrels scurried off from the accident scene and took up residence in a nearby pecan grove.

The farmer eventually scooped up two of the critters and sent them to live with his niece in Brevard. She kept them inside as pets hoping the snow-kissed rodents might breed. No such luck. Eventually one escaped and the other was released. Despite their lack of amorous success in captivity white squirrels soon began appearing around town. Or so the story goes.

The white squirrels are not pigment-starved albinos as they boast dark beady eyes. Other towns claim fealty to their white squirrels but those imposters are bred from albinos. Botanists do not recognize a distinct species of white squirrels and these are probably the offspring of hooking up with gray squirrels. The gray squirrel is the official State Mammal of North Carolina but the folks in Brevard go way beyond that - in 1986 the city council declared the entirety of the city a sanctuary for all squirrels - gray, white or in between. Today squirrel census counters estimate that more than 25% of all the squirrels scurrying around Brevard are white.

All squirrels are revered in Brevard but special hosannas are reserved for the white squirrels that scurry about the town.

One of the best places to spot one of these rascals is on the leafy campus of Brevard College. One time of year you are guaranteed to spot the rare breed is during the White Squirrel Festival. There is music, a parade, headlining bands, and a Squirrel Box Derby competition down Jailhouse Hill. And always in attendance is Pisgah Pete, a rescued white squirrel.

Lake Lure

Although you would be hard pressed to tell it by looking at Western North Carolina's most beautiful lake, the man-made body of water was created in 1927 to generate electricity. The town followed. But before that, dial the Wayback machine to the 1800s and the granite monolith of Chimney Rock. Missourian Lucius B. Morse was captivated with the big rock in the Hickory Nut Gorge from the first time he came to the Blue Ridge Mountains for the restorative air to ease his tuberculosis. Morse and two brothers bought 64 acres around Chimney Rock in 1902 and set out to improve tourist access to his rock.

Morse eventually had 8,000 acres, many of which were submerged by the damming of the quick-stepping Rocky Broad River. The lake supports a resort community whose visitors dwarf the thousand or so permanent residents. In addition to fun on the water, Lake Lure boasts a unique Flowering Bridge and the best beach for Ashevillians.

High Time to Visit

DIRTY DANCING FESTIVAL
AUGUST

Movie fans of a certain age all know the Kellerman Resort, the summer getaway in New York's Catskills Mountains where Patrick Swayze and Jennifer Gray fell in love in 1987's *Dirty Dancing*. The film crew, however, never went anywhere near the Empire State. Most of the movie was filmed at the Mountain Lake

After the historic 1925 bridge over the Rocky Broad River was closed in 2011 the three-arch span was converted into a native flower garden.

71

Hotel in Virginia and in Lake Lure to portray 1964. There isn't much to see of the filming locations anymore - many of the cabins at the Chimney Rock Camp for Boys were torn down, the gymnasium and dining hall burned down and the bridge where Baby learns to dance was ripped apart by souvenir hunters. None of that deters the organizers of the Dirty Dancing Festival which includes an outdoor screening of the movie, plenty of dancing with the help of the Asheville Ballet, a lake-lift competition and watermelon carrying races (if you've seen the movie you don't have to ask).

Hot Springs

There is only one known thermal spring in North Carolina and it is 45 minutes north of Asheville. James Patton created one of the state's first resorts here in 1831. It was only Warm Springs then, when he built a 350-room hotel with 13 large columns - one for each of the original

The Mountain Park Hotel was among the most luxurious in Western North Carolina in its heyday, with 1000 feet of piazzas. It burned in 1920.

colonies. After that hotel burned an even grander tourist palace replaced it in the 1880s and an even hotter mineral spring was discovered so the town's name was upgraded to Hot Springs. It burned too, and so did two more replacements. The springs are now operated as a private outdoor spa and the town, which was used as an internment camp during World War I, is now an historic district.

High Time to Visit

FRENCH BROAD RIVER FESTIVAL
MAY

The French Broad River is mostly tame as it makes its way through Asheville but as it rambles to the Holston River to form the Tennessee River in Knoxville it gains in character. Near Hot Springs the river is producing Class II and Class III rapids, enough of a whitewater experience to get the pulse racing while remaining a family experience. This is Section 9 of the French Broad River and has been an aquatic racetrack since Cherokee times. For the festival the Southeast's biggest mass start whitewater race launches nine miles upstream in Barnard and concludes in the middle of a full-bore weekend party.

If you can't relax in Hot Springs, you aren't trying.

Epilogue

Have you got all that? Now go out and be an Ashevillian.

Made in the USA
Middletown, DE
15 December 2017